Sarah's Journey

Alan D. Wolfelt, Ph.D.
Director, Center for Loss and Life Transition

Illustrated by Lori Mackey

Other Publications by Alan D. Wolfelt, Ph.D.

A Child's View of Grief

*What Bereaved Children Want Adults
to Know About Grief*

*Creating Meaningful Funeral Ceremonies:
A Guide for Caregivers*

*Healing the Bereaved Child:
Grief Gardening, ·
Growth Through Grief and
Other Touchstones for Caregivers*

*The Journey Through Grief:
Reflections on Healing*

Understanding Grief: Helping Yourself Heal

Companion Press is an imprint of the
Center for Loss and Life Transition,
3735 Broken Bow Road, Fort Collins, Colorado 80526

Printed in the United States of America

07 06 05 04 03 02 01 00 99 98   7 6 5 4 3
ISBN: 1-879651-03-3

Contents

Preface

Eight-year-old Sarah Johnson had always been her "daddy's little girl." Sarah loved him very much. One day, Sarah's father was killed in a tragic automobile accident, and her life changed forever.

Sarah's Journey: One Child's Experience With The Death of Her Father is a walk through three years of Sarah's life after her father's death. The book describes Sarah's personal grief experience through individual narratives of her life, followed in each chapter by "A Counselor's Perspective" and "Guidelines For Caring Adults." Originally published as a series of articles in *Bereavement Magazine,* this book is a response to readers' positive comments and interest in the topic of childhood grief.

Children like Sarah are often referred to as the "forgotten mourners." They grieve inwardly but are often not able, or permitted, to mourn. By clinical definition, mourning is the outward sharing of the thoughts and feelings about the death and the person who has died. My goal in *Sarah's Journey* is to validate children's need and right to mourn and to assist caring adults who wish to help children do so in life-enhancing ways.

The book covers the various dimensions of grief, including regressive behavior, explosive emotions, acting out, and the "Big-Man"/"Big-Woman" Syndrome, which are all common, and natural, responses by children to the death of someone loved.

Sarah's Journey also provides information about the value for children of a funeral or some type of ritual and how school personnel can be of assistance to bereaved children in the school environment.

Throughout *Sarah's Journey,* I refer to Sarah as "teaching me" about her grief experience. The counseling model I use when working with bereaved children is that they know best what their own personal grief experiences are like. As caring adults and professional caregivers, our job is to listen to what they have to say — and to learn from them. Our job is never to prescribe what a child should be thinking or feeling following the death of someone loved.

I urge you to bring to this book a desire to truly

understand what the grief experience may be like for a child. As you read the words, open your head and your heart to what it is like from a child's perspective.

Alan D. Wolfelt, Ph.D.
Center For Loss and Life Transition
Fort Collins, Colorado

I
Sarah's
Journey
Begins

Eight-year-old Sarah Johnson had always
been known as "Daddy's little girl." The
youngest of three children, she loved her father
very much. She often waited on the front porch
as the time neared for Dad to come home from

work.

On weekends, Dad and Sarah always guarded what they both called "our special time" — two hours every Saturday afternoon when they shared activities together. Sometimes they would go to the park and feed the ducks or sometimes they rode bikes together. At other times, they would simply sit and visit.

Just last Saturday, Sarah and Dad had gone to the mountains, where, hand in hand, they hiked trails together. They enjoyed watching the deer feed and actually came within only a few feet of a newborn fawn. Sarah and Dad smiled at each other and laughed, both realizing how much fun it was to be together.

After school the following Wednesday afternoon, Sarah's life changed forever. As she approached the house she had always lived in with her parents and older brothers, she knew something was wrong — terribly wrong. A stream of cars was pulling up to the house, and several neighbors with sad faces were standing in the driveway. With some uncertainty, she slowly moved toward the front door. As they saw her approaching, the neighbors stood quietly, saying nothing and staring with a penetrating and frightening silence.

Her Uncle Bill met her at the door, took her by the hand and led her into the main living area. Sarah's mother was across the room, head bowed, not saying a word to the half-dozen people surrounding her. When Mrs. Johnson saw Sarah, she broke into tears and reached out to embrace her daughter.

Mom cried as she held Sarah as tight as she possibly could. Sarah didn't say anything as she began to search the room for her beloved father. After a few minutes, Sarah forced out three words she will always remember: "Where's my daddy?" With the exception of Mom's muffled tears, the room suddenly became totally silent.

Several more minutes had passed when Sarah's favorite grandpa bent down, and while comforting both mother and child, said, "Sarah, we have some very sad news to tell you. Your daddy was in a car accident today, and he has died. The ambulance people tried to save him, but they couldn't."

Sarah's mind and body seemed to shut down all at once. She couldn't think, she couldn't feel, she couldn't do. As Mom cried, and Grandpa comforted, not a single tear rolled down Sarah's cheek. Her only way of surviving the moment was to 'not feel' right now.

Suddenly, and without hesitation, Sarah announced, "I'm going out in the backyard to play." She slowly pulled herself away from her mother's arms, walked through the kitchen and out the back door. Without knowing why or how, her legs and feet got her there. She walked to a sandbox that she hadn't used for at least a year, sat down right in the middle and started to build a castle. Again, not knowing why, she began to sing "Jingle Bells," her favorite Christmas song. As she played in the sand and sang her song, Sarah thought quietly to herself, "My daddy's not dead, he'll come back."

Within the next hour, more people arrived at the house to offer their care and presence. The phone was beginning to ring continuously as friends and family reached out to help the Johnson family. Food was brought in and family members drove in from throughout the state.

Two hours had passed since Sarah's arrival home from school. Family members kept *checking on her out in the backyard as she was joined in play by her brothers and several cousins. Mostly, Sarah sat in the sandbox singing songs and smiling at her playmates.*

At one point, Sarah's Aunt Mary looked out the kitchen window to watch the children at play. Seeing Sarah smiling, laughing and playing, she turned to other adults in the room and said, "Look, just as I thought; Sarah is really too young to understand what's happening. Besides, I knew she could be strong. Don't you all think it would just be best if I took her over to my house until the funeral is over? I don't think we should make her go through all that."

Not ten minutes later, Uncle Fred looked out to see Sarah playing in the sandbox. In a quick manner and loud tone, he said to other family members, "Doesn't Sarah realize what's going on?! She shouldn't be playing; she should be crying. Didn't she love her father? I think we should get her in here and sit her down on the couch. Let's make her realize what a tragic day this is."

As Sarah continued to play, sing and even smile, she began to wonder inside herself when

Daddy would come home from work. After all, she reasoned, all our friends and family are here — Daddy should be here too. She paused to catch her breath, and as she exhaled, a single tear slowly rolled down her cheek. She didn't understand her tear, but she knew something was wrong—terribly wrong!

A Counselor's Perspective. . .

As Sarah plays in the sandbox, some of the adults observing her decide that she is "too young to understand" and needs to be protected from the experiences surrounding the death. The watchful eyes of other adults imply that Sarah should almost "be punished" for not having more of an outwardly sad emotional response.

As is often the situation with children, Sarah's initial response to the death of her father is emotional shock and apparent lack of feelings. A child often reasons, "If I pretend this isn't happening, then maybe it won't be." Disbelief and numbness are nature's way of caring for children. After all, a child's head level of thinking and heart level of feeling are very different. Many children discover there are no adequate words to describe this initial period of intense grief.

Sometimes adults observing the child from the outside are quick to conclude that shock, disbelief, numbness, and apparent lack of feeling mean total and complete denial of the death. With responsive guidance, however, children like Sarah are able to allow enough reality through to pace their journey into grief. According to their own needs, they move toward their grief instead of away from it. As they approach the emotional reality, children will often do some "catch-up grieving" as thoughts and feelings surface that previously were blocked from full consciousness.

Adults frequently have difficulty understanding how the child can be out in the backyard playing only moments after learning of a loved person's death. Yet, what may seem to be a lack of feeling is frequently the child's attempt at self-protection.

Often confusing to children like Sarah is that this apparent lack of feeling is sometimes viewed as a positive, long-term response to the death. In our culture, some people unfortunately advocate facing trauma without showing any feeling. As Aunt Mary said, "I knew she could be strong." The person who does not cry when someone dies is often the one who others believe "took things so well."

To a child, the messages are mixed. Some adults give the child a message to "be strong," or, "you are too young to understand;" other adults simply cannot conceive why the child is not mourning. They ask themselves if the child really loved the person who died. As Uncle Fred said, "Didn't she love her father?" The result — many children, Sarah included, frequently get stuck in the middle not knowing what to think, feel, or do.

Guidelines for Caring Adults

◆ **Accept the child's apparent lack of feelings as a natural response.**
The major role of the "helping-healing adult" during this time of disbelief and apparent lack of feeling is to keep the child in touch with a supportive, caring part of the world. Acceptance of this natural, yet temporary, protective mechanism is an important step toward healing.

- **Talk "with," not "at," the child about the death.**

  The tendency to talk "at" instead of "with" a bereaved child is often a reflection of the adult's sense of helplessness. If adults recognize this tendency, they can help prevent it from occurring. And remember — a quiet and stabilizing presence is frequently more comforting than the content of any words.

- **Respect the child's need to talk, or not to talk, about the death.**

  Caring adults must learn to respect a child's need to move in and out of grief. Most bereaved children will provide cues as to when they feel comfortable and safe talking about the person who has died. A child will often test adults to see if they feel comfortable communicating their thoughts and feelings about the loss. As adults build a relationship based on sensitivity, warmth, and under-standing, children will feel more comfortable sharing their grief.

A child cannot be forced to mourn; however, he or she can be permitted and encouraged to do so as timing and pacing allow. Adults who expect more from a child early in the experience of a new loss may be meeting their own needs as opposed to the needs of the child. Children must have opportunities to mourn in healthy ways, but should never be forced to feel something before their hearts are ready to be open to the pain that precedes healing. Just as band-aids protect a fresh physical wound, a child may need to cover up a severe emotional wound as well.

II
Sarah
Responds
To Her
Loss

When we left Sarah, she was quietly playing in her sandbox. While time seemed to stand still, she had managed to build a sand castle right in the middle of her imaginary world. Months later, she would describe her sand castle as "a big house with a mom, dad and three happy

children who lived happily ever after."

As daytime turned to darkness, Grandpa called the children into the house. One by one, the children inched closer to the back door. Not wanting to budge from the security of her sandbox, Sarah continued to smile and sing. After all, staying where she was helped slow down her world.

Another twenty minutes passed, yet Sarah remained outside, not wanting to confront the beginning of a new reality. Perhaps part of her knew that her daddy was dead, but her mind and body kept saying, "No, it can't be!"

Her grandpa walked to her side and gently took her hand. Together they silently entered the house. Sarah moved through the kitchen into the living room where she went to the large picture window. Pressing her forehead to the glass, she peered outside and down the street — watching and waiting.

People around Sarah seemed uncertain of what to say or do. After only a few minutes, Sarah turned away from the window and began to look for her mother. Without uttering a word, she moved through the house in search of Mom.

The house was full of friends and family, yet no one spoke to Sarah as she searched.

Turning from the hallway into a large bedroom, Sarah found Mom lying on the bed. A wide-awake Mrs. Johnson seemed oblivious to the sound of voices that filtered through the house. Without hesitation, Sarah snuggled up to Mom and held her as tight as strength would allow.

Mom held Sarah in her arms as she softly whispered, "I love you Sarah . . . I love you so very much." Sarah asked Mom to rock her and hold her as close as she could. Mrs. Johnson willingly pulled Sarah even closer. Sarah responded, "I love you, too, Mom. I love you, too."

Rocking, holding, hugging each other — tears came for both Sarah and her mother. Kleenex tissues sat on a nearby table, yet they felt no need to reach out for any. Neither Sarah nor Mom had any desire to stop the crying. While there was pain in the tears, there was also comfort in their shared togetherness.

In the following weeks and months, Sarah would want Mom to hold and rock her many more times. She would also occasionally talk "baby talk," or find herself having difficulty being separated from Mom. These were only a few of a number of behaviors Sarah would express in her effort to be nurtured, reassured, and loved.

A Counselor's Perspective. . .

Under the normal stress of grief, children often return to a sense of protection and security experienced at earlier times in life. Clinically, this pattern is referred to as "regressive behavior." Some of the more common regressive behaviors in children who are in mourning include the following:

— Desiring to be nursed or rocked.

— Expressing difficulty being separated from parents or other significant adults.

— Requesting that other people perform simple tasks, such as tying shoes, dressing, or feeding, that the child was previously capable of doing alone.

— Demonstrating difficulty working independently at school.

— Searching for constant, individual

22

attention.

— Adopting a "sick role" in an effort to be nurtured.

— Fearing the dark.

— Talking "baby talk," and, in general, becoming an infant requiring care.

During times of loss and transition, even adults wish to return to an earlier developmental level. If children are allowed to return to simpler, safer times while experiencing the pain of their grief, they will often emerge more competent as they do the work of mourning in healthy ways. Unfortunately, some adults interpret regressive behaviors as showing a lack of self control. The result — bereaved children may be discouraged from, or even punished for, retreating into the security of earlier times.

Guidelines for Caring Adults

◆ **Allow the child to retreat to a safer, less complex time; this behavior after the death of someone loved is natural.** Regressive behaviors in a bereaved child are usually temporary and pass as he or she is supported in the journey into grief. An understanding of the natural and temporary nature of this behavior allows adults to respond with sensitivity and love during this critical time.

A return to prior developmental levels can take place at any time during the child's grief experience. These behaviors, however, tend to be even more noticeable immediately following the death.

+ **Remember that demonstrating regressive behavior may fill a significant need in the bereaved child's life. Be patient and understanding.**

Temporary, self-preserving regression undoubtedly serves a useful purpose for many bereaved children. It signals a need to be cared for, nurtured, and loved. Regressive behavior may also represent an attempt to return to a time in life before the trauma of the loss; it may even be a way for the child to retrieve the person who has died.

+ **Provide a trusting, supportive presence for the child.**

Perhaps an adult's helping efforts are best served by providing a trusting, supportive presence that allows the child to share his or her conflicting thoughts and feelings without fear of judgment. For children, to regress is simply to ask for "care-eliciting" behaviors from adults around them.

The child who is not allowed to regress, or worse yet is punished for regressing, will often bury the pain of grief inside. Yet when these conflicts and pains are expressed openly, it is easier for a child to move forward in healthy, life-enhancing ways.

As Sarah and her mother held each other tightly, they were beginning the long and difficult process of acknowledging that their family was forever changed. It would not be until much later that both mother and daughter would understand that all of life's hurts ultimately involve pulling backward before moving forward. Fortunately, Sarah was allowing herself the necessity of slowing down and being nurtured by someone she loved very much.

III
Sarah
Learns About
The Meaning
Of A
Funeral

Sarah was holding her mother as closely
as she possibly could. With her head snuggled
tightly against Mom's chest, Sarah drifted off
into a deep, yet restless, sleep. She hoped that
she might awake the next morning to discover

the news of Daddy's death was only a terrible dream.

As mother and daughter tried to sleep, well-meaning friends and family members began to discuss what they thought would be best regarding the funeral. Circled around the kitchen table, opinions included the following:

Aunt Mary: "Well, I think we should just get the funeral over. It will be too hard for everyone."

Uncle Fred: "Maybe we should just go into the funeral home and make the arrangements for the family."

Grandpa: "Perhaps we should just slow down and let this family decide what will best meet their needs."

Sarah awoke early the next morning still clinging to the security of her mother's arms. As she peered out through her swollen red eyes, the reality of her beloved father's death still seemed impossible. Months would pass before Sarah would fully understand that Daddy could not come home.

Hand-in-hand, Mom led Sarah to the room of her oldest brother. Thirteen-year-old Chris and eleven-year-old Jeff were sitting together in a calm, almost mystical, silence. Both boys had wanted to be alone with their personal grief for a period of time. Only this morning had all four remaining members of the Johnson family come together to acknowledge that at least some comfort came from being in each other's presence.

Sarah was glad to see her brothers with whom she shared a special closeness. Not a word was said as mother and daughter joined the boys who were sitting in the middle of the floor. Chris reached out and touched Sarah on the elbow as Mom pulled Jeff close to her.

The silence went unbroken until Mrs. Johnson slowly and softly spoke the following words: "This is very painful for all of us right now. . . and I might say and do some crazy things in the days and weeks ahead. We all loved your father very much."

As she paused to catch her breath, Chris looked directly into his mom's eyes and said, "He loved you too, Mom — he loved you too." As Mom allowed herself to cry, she said nothing directly back to Chris, yet her facial expression acknowledged that she understood his warm and caring message.

Mrs. Johnson continued, "I may not have answers to some of your questions right now — I don't even have answers to my own questions. If I can't help you because of what is going on inside me, I'll see that Grandpa and others will be close to you. Daddy loved you, and I still love you. I hope that together all of us can plan a funeral and remember what a good person he always was."

Mom's openness made it comfortable for Sarah to decide that she wanted to be a part of planning for Dad's funeral. She wasn't forced to participate, but she was encouraged to be involved in the difficult, yet necessary process. Part of Sarah still wanted to run away and hide — reasoning that if she could just go far away, none of this would be happening.

Only an hour before the family was to leave for the funeral home, Sarah searched out and found her favorite grandpa in the side yard. As she approached him, he met her with open arms. Drawing herself close she whispered into his ear, "Grandpa, why do we have funerals?"

Grandpa asked Sarah to sit on his lap, and in a kind and gentle voice, he patiently answered her question. "Sarah, when someone we love dies, we are sad and we hurt all over. Having a funeral allows people to come together and comfort each other. This helps with some of our sadness. It also helps us remember that others care too." He paused, wanting to see that Sarah was supported by his response.

Being certain not to make his response too long, and to involve Sarah, he continued. "You know what a good feeling it was to love your daddy?" Sarah nodded in agreement as she watched her grandpa carefully. "Your love for him didn't end when he died in that car accident yesterday. The funeral will help us share the love we have for your daddy. We are going to have a special time to remember the happy and good times he brought to our lives. I guess we could say that we are going to honor and remember your dad for all the love he gave to us."

Following a long, quiet pause Sarah asked, "Will we say a prayer at the funeral, Grandpa?"

"Yes, Sarah, our hope and belief in God will also be a part of the funeral."

While some well-meaning friends and relatives objected, Mrs. Johnson decided that the children were an integral part of making the funeral a meaningful experience. The comforting presence of Grandpa was also a welcome addition to this loving family.

The planning was completed on Thursday afternoon. The group decided that the family would receive friends on Friday afternoon and evening, and the service would be held Saturday morning at 10:00 a.m. A special family time was reserved for Friday morning.

On Friday morning, Sarah, Mom, her two brothers and Grandpa slowly walked down a hallway that opened into the chapel of the funeral home. They walked this same path yesterday as Mr. Stephens, the funeral director, had prepared the family for where Daddy's body would be during the visitation and funeral. Grandpa and Mr. Stephens had worked together to prepare the children for what they would see and do at the funeral home.

As they entered the chapel, Sarah firmly grasped her mother's hand. Thirty feet away, she could see her Daddy in the oak casket she had helped pick out. Not a word was spoken as, arm-in-arm, the family approached a reality they wished would go away. Mom was the first to allow herself to openly cry and cry. Sarah, Jeff, and Grandpa followed with tears of their own, while oldest brother Chris turned and walked away into a distant corner of the room. As time passed, the Johnson family supported each other in their shared grief.

Sarah would later comment, "Seeing Daddy made me know he really died." The funeral director had explained to Mrs. Johnson that when a death is sudden and unexpected, the need to confront the reality of the body often becomes very important to survivors.

While part of Sarah's mother wanted to protect the children from any and all pain, she too would later reflect, "Seeing Brad's body was something I really struggled with. Part of me wanted to run away and hide. Only now have I come to understand that, for our family, seeing him was part of saying goodbye and making his death believable."

Hundreds of family members and friends came to the funeral home to support the

Johnsons and to say their own good-byes to Sarah's dad. Sarah found that at times she needed some time away from the large crowd of people. The funeral home had a "children's room" that was full of toys and games, and she found herself coming and going from this room throughout the day. On one occasion, the funeral director sat in the room with her and answered questions that Sarah needed answered.

Mr. Stephens could answer most of Sarah's questions; however, one question needed not only an explanation, but a demonstration. It seems that Sarah's seven-year-old cousin, Katy, had asked her, "What happened to your Daddy's legs?" Katy had seen the half-open casket and, as many children will, assumed that only half of Mr. Johnson was in the casket.

The funeral director responded to Sarah, "Sometimes people think that only half of the person is there. If you want, we can open the bottom part and show you your Daddy's legs." Sarah thought this was a good idea and went to get her cousin Katy. The two young girls met Mr. Stephens beside the casket and he opened the *bottom portion of the lid. Standing hand-in-hand, Sarah and Katy now understood and walked off to return to the playroom.*

The funeral service itself will always be remembered by Sarah and her family. Their church pastor made a special effort to personalize his message and share specific memories of how Mr. Johnson had touched people's lives. Sarah and her brothers each told Reverend Newby of their own unique and memorable times with their father.

Of course, for Sarah, her special Saturday time with Dad was always going to be a unique memory. The pastor acknowledged this important time between father and daughter and then went on to explain, "If any of you ever had the privilege of seeing Brad with his daughter, Sarah, you know what a wonderful relationship these two had. Just this past spring I ran into them at the city park. All they were doing was feeding ducks, but I've never seen a parent and child so outwardly enjoying the love they had for each other."

With Grandpa on one side of her and Mom on the other, Sarah heard these words and quietly allowed tears to roll down her cheeks as she recalled so many happy times with her daddy.

At a point toward the end of the service, Reverend Newby paused and explained, "Last night, Sarah handed me a poem by Dorothy Law Nolte that she knew was very special to her father. Brad had this poem framed and on his desk at home. I don't think Sarah would mind if I shared this poem with you this morning. As I read it, perhaps we can all remember what a wonderful father this man was to children.

Children Learn What They Live

If children live with criticism,
They learn to condemn.
If children live with hostility,
They learn to fight.
If children live with ridicule,
They learn to be shy.
If children live with shame,
They learn to feel guilty.
If children live with tolerance,
They learn to be patient.
If children live with encouragement,
They learn confidence.
If children live with praise,
They learn to appreciate.
If children live with fairness,
They learn justice.
If children live with security,
They learn to have faith.
If children live with approval,
They learn to like themselves.
If children live with acceptance and friendship,
They learn to find love in the world.

At the conclusion of the funeral, the pastor returned the poem to Sarah as he gave her a big hug. Without hesitation, Sarah took a pen from her mother's purse and wrote in capital letters across the poem: I WILL ALWAYS LOVE YOU, DADDY. After signing her name, she placed these words that meant so much to her dad beside him in the casket.

Without a doubt, Sarah's daddy and best friend had helped her live with encouragement, acceptance, friendship, and maybe most of all, LOVE. These qualities he conveyed to Sarah will forever be a part of her. Through the funeral experience and the sharing of their pain, hurt and hope, the Johnson family began the initial steps toward healing.

A Counselor's Perspective. . .

Sarah and her family experienced first-hand the positive impact of planning and attending the funeral of someone loved who has died. A funeral, or some type of ritual, is important to the persons left behind. Why? The following reasons help answer that question:

— Funerals provide a structure to support and

assist family and friends through their initial period of mourning.

— Funerals provide a time to honor, remember, and affirm the life of the person who has died.

— Funerals allow for a "search for meaning" within the context of each person's religious or philosophical values or beliefs.

— Funerals help acknowledge and confirm that someone loved has died.

— Funerals allow a focus for the natural expression of thoughts and feelings about the loss.

— Funerals are a time to remember the person who died and help mourners move gently from having a "relationship of presence" to a "relationship of memory" with that loved one.

— Funerals give testimony to the value of life and living and acknowledge that the life of the person who died had meaning and purpose.

— Funerals are a time to say "thank you" for having had the privilege of knowing and caring about the person who has died.

Perhaps most importantly, funerals are a means of socially acknowledging that the lives of those persons left behind will be forever changed — a significant loss has occurred and life will never be quite the same as it was before the person died.

IV
After The Funeral: Sarah Returns To School

The funeral was over. As Mr. Johnson's body was lowered into the grave, this young family was confronted with the reality that their lives were forever changed. Sarah will always remember how Mr. Stephens, the funeral director, handed her a single red rose from the

spray of casket flowers.

Following the service, people gathered at the family home as they continued to support and comfort each other. Sarah had never seen so much food in all of her life! Grandpa helped her understand that bringing food was one way that people expressed their love for the family.

Eight-year-old Sarah would later remember how some of what was happening seemed to be fun — all the food, pretty flowers, people not just crying, but sometimes laughing. One day, she will probably learn the sad reality that sometimes the only time family members see each other is at weddings and funerals.

At one point she privately asked her grandpa, "Why are people laughing?" Slowly and calmly, Grandpa explained, "Well, you see Sarah, most of these people haven't seen each other in a long time. They are glad to see each other so they sometimes talk and laugh. But, you have also seen them crying. It's kind of confusing, but their laughing doesn't mean they didn't love your daddy. They loved him very much." Grandpa's response provoked an unsuspecting comment from Sarah. She asked, "You mean it's okay that

I had some fun in the playroom at the funeral home? Uncle Fred told me to sit and be quiet, but I just couldn't." Understanding Sarah's question, Grandpa reassured her, "Sarah, just like you see these people laughing and talking, you can't just be quiet and not move around. Moving around, playing, and talking, all help us right now."

A look of relief came over Sarah's face. Only later would other adults around the Johnson children learn that "moving around" and "being in contact with the world outside of oneself" was actually a way of surviving the trauma. Grandpa was aware that many grieving children speed up their activity levels following a major loss.

By the following evening, family and friends began to return to their own homes. Now, for the first time since the tragic death of their loving father and husband, Sarah, her mom, and two brothers were alone.

Grandpa was the last one to leave on that Sunday night. Months later, Sarah would remember wishing he could stay. In her mind, and perhaps in reality, she needed Grandpa to comfort her, to hold her, and to make her world seem safe. She knew by now that not many people around her had the "healing gifts" of her cherished grandpa.

On his way out the door, Grandpa reached out to embrace Sarah one more time. Words seemed unnecessary as Sarah and Grandpa held each other tight. Three tears rolled down her cheeks as she wondered to herself, "What would I do without my grandpa?" A smile broke through the tears as she leaned in closer and kissed him goodbye.

The week that followed was full of activities for Sarah and her family. Sarah and eleven-year-old Jeff decided to stay home from school for a few more days while thirteen-year-old Chris opted to go right back to school. The telephone was ringing almost constantly the first week. One afternoon, Mrs. Johnson took the telephone off the hook and explained to the children, "It's nice that people care and want to help, but maybe we can just have some quiet time for a few hours." Sarah remembers being comforted by the "quiet time" which she spent snuggled up between her brother Jeff and Mom.

On Tuesday evening, the two boys and Sarah went with Mrs. Johnson to select a monument for Dad's grave. A family friend drove them, and Sarah sat in the front seat with her mother. About halfway to their destination, Jeff broke the silence, "Mom, I think I want to go back to school tomorrow." Listening closely, Sarah also spoke up, "Me too . . . I miss my friends." Mrs. Johnson nodded as she stared blankly out the front of the windshield. Tomorrow, Jeff and Sarah would return to school.

At 8:00 a.m. the next morning, Sarah walked through the door of her third grade classroom. It was exactly one week ago today that her world fell apart. Returning to a familiar place with friends and a caring teacher seemed a welcome relief.

Sarah's teacher, Mrs. Miller, was a warm, compassionate person who had a close relationship with all of her students. At the funeral, she had hand-delivered a homemade sympathy card the class created for Sarah. The card was made out of a small box that could be opened. Inside the box was a separate note to Sarah from each student in her class. This box of notes was very special to Sarah, and she had a specific place in her bedroom to keep it.

Sarah will always remember the note from her best friend, Laura. It read,

> *Dear Sarah,*
>
> *I'm sorry your daddy died. He was a really nice person. My mommy and daddy liked him a lot. Everyone at my house cried when we found out. Why do people die? Nobody will tell me. I just want to know. I sure don't want to do it.*
>
> *Your Best Friend,*
>
> *Laura.*

Mrs. Miller was aware that while bereaved children's lives are forever changed, they need to feel their relationships are secure. While striving to be a stabilizer and comforter, she took precautions not to be overly solicitous to Sarah. Mrs. Miller knew that to adopt an attitude of "Oh, you poor child," would only be destructive to Sarah's ultimate well-being. Mrs. Miller also knew that in supporting and providing opportunities for Sarah to mourn, she could become a "helping-healing" adult.

Perhaps this caring teacher's personal letter

to Sarah best illustrated her kind and focused effort to help:

> *Dear Sarah:*
>
> *I'm thinking and praying for you and your family. Your daddy was a kind and gentle man. I know he loved you with all his heart.*
>
> *Everyone at school is thinking of you and will be glad when you come back to class. We can talk if you want to talk, and we can sit together if you want to sit. I'll be here for you and so will all your friends.*
>
> *Your teacher,*
>
> *Mrs. Miller*

Yes, Sarah was glad to be back, and her classmates and teacher were glad to have her back. Everyone knew that Sarah's world was vastly changed from one week ago today. But, what they didn't know, was that tucked away in her back-pack on her first day's return to school was that special box of caring notes from her friends and teacher.

A Counselor's Perspective. . .

Sarah welcomed her return to school. The familiar faces and the kind words of her fellow students and her teacher provided a stabilizing influence in her world, which had so recently been turned upside down. Sarah's teacher, Mrs. Miller, was particularly aware of the need to be sensitive and understanding at this critical time.

As Mrs. Miller demonstrated, death education for teachers has become a reality. Responsible guidance by a caring adult in the school setting is an important part of helping a child heal from the emotional wounds caused by the death of someone loved.

For readers of this book who are teachers, the following guidelines may be helpful if one of your students has experienced a loss similar to Sarah's.

1. Explore your personal attitudes and experiences related to death. To help your grieving student, you must also examine your own thoughts and feelings about death.

2. Continually enhance your own knowledge about childhood grief. While you will never know absolutely "everything there is to know about death," strive to broaden your understanding about this complex issue. Many school districts across the country

now provide resources and death education workshops for teachers.

3. When a death impacts your school, understand individual and group needs. From my experience as a grief counselor, I know you will find a wide variety of responses, concerns, and questions from adults as well as children.

4. Create active listening and sharing opportunities surrounding death. Perhaps nothing is more important than providing the time and space for children to express their grief openly.

5. Reach out for help when you think it seems appropriate. While no one person or profession has all the "answers," there is no substitute for cooperatively working with parents, fellow teachers, counselors, physicians, and clergy to meet the needs of bereaved children.

6. Remember the concepts of the "teachable moment" and the "created moment." The teachable moment is when an opportunity arises to instruct children about life through events that occur around them. A pet may

die, or a classmate's parent (as in Sarah's experience) may die. When these events occur, use the opportunity to talk openly about your students' thoughts and feelings about it. The created moment means don't wait for "one-big-tell-all" about death; work to create opportunities to teach children about death in relation to life.

7. Communicate openly and honestly. Express your own feelings about death, being careful not to project the idea that everyone should feel the same way. Provide children with a model for expressing their own feelings — whatever those feelings might be.

8. Keep in mind that no one procedure or formula will fit all children in all classrooms, either at the time of death or during the months that follow. Be patient, flexible, and adjust to individual needs.

9. Work to enhance your knowledge not only of what to do for grieving children, but also what not to do. For example, associating death with sleep, saying that somebody has gone on a long trip, or implying that death is some form of punishment are definitely

not comments to share with a bereaved child.

10. Occasionally remind yourself of the old saying: "The mediocre teacher tells, the good teacher explains, the superior teacher demonstrates, and the great teacher inspires." As a caring adult in the classroom, you can not only teach children about death, but inspire them about life.

V
Sarah And Her Family Do The Work Of Mourning

As the Johnson family tried to return to some semblance of a normal routine, Sarah, Chris, Jeff, and Mom all knew that life was forever changed. The tragic car accident that took the life of their loving father and husband seemed so unfair. As a tearful relative had expressed at the funeral, "These things are supposed to happen in someone else's family, not your own!"

Now that the three children had all returned to school, Mrs. Johnson was discovering that she was ambivalent about the moments she now had for herself. She was relieved to sometimes be alone, yet time seemed so distorted. Minutes seemed like hours, and hours seemed like days. The Johnson family would later understand that the pain of acute grief creates a distorted sense of both time and space in most mourners.

Sarah and her two brothers, Chris and Jeff, were expressing grief from Dad's death in their own unique ways. While Sarah and Jeff were, at times, outwardly verbally expressive with their grief, thirteen-year-old Chris was experiencing the "Big Man Syndrome."

Within two weeks after his father's death, Chris began to act like the "man of the house." Of course, he was simply following the instructions of many well-intended, yet misinformed, adults.

At the funeral, several adults had approached Chris with messages that encouraged this grown-up behavior. Among the comments were the following: "Chris, you are going to have a lot of responsibility in your family now;" "Be sure to take good care of your little brother and sister;" and "You need to be the man of the house now that your dad is not here."

In an effort to live up to these expectations, ten days after his father's death, Chris announced to his mother that he had dropped off the school football team. When questioned about his reasons for quitting, Chris responded,

"I need to be at home to watch over things."
Naturally overwhelmed by her own grief, Mom
didn't have the energy to pursue her son's
reasoning.

Without any history of a past role as
disciplinarian in the family, Chris also began
to constantly inform Jeff and Sarah of what to
do and what not to do. On one occasion, he
actually informed Sarah that she was grounded
for not cleaning her room.

And early on a Saturday morning after the
funeral, Mom discovered Chris out in the garage
attempting to change the oil in the family car.
When asked what he was doing, Chris answered
in an angry voice, "I'm doing what I'm
supposed to be doing — the jobs that Dad used
to do."

A Counselor's Perspective. . .

Chris, like thousands of other bereaved
children, took the messages to heart. He
internalized the belief that to be a "good boy"
meant to become a "big man." The sad,
sometimes tragic reality is that striving to be the
"big man" frequently results in a frustrated,

depressed child or adolescent.

When a child (usually the oldest and the same-sex child as the parent who died) attempts to grow up quickly, it is formally defined as the "Big Man" or "Big Woman" syndrome. Some of these children are simply carrying out the instructions of respected adults who are well-intended, but unaware of the potentially damaging, long-term impact of their messages.

Some children unconsciously may also adopt the "Big Man" or "Big Woman" syndrome as a symbolic means of trying to keep the dead person alive. If the roles filled by the dead parent continue, it is as if the family doesn't have to acknowledge the full impact of how life has changed. In addition, this forced hyper-maturity can be the child's means of protection from a feeling of hopelessness and helplessness in the grief journey. In similar fashion, some bereaved children will even attempt to ease the surviving parent's grief by trying to fill the gaps left by the dead parent.

As illustrated by Chris, some children will attempt to care for and discipline other children in the family. Naturally consumed by their own grief, surviving parents often find comfort in someone else's willingness to provide discipline. They may lack both the energy and desire to provide appropriate behavioral limits. This situation is particularly the case when the dead spouse previously served as the primary disciplinarian in the family.

In the Johnson family, Dad was the disciplinarian. While Mom and Dad had shared in some of the responsibility for discipline, Mr. Johnson always was the one to enforce any final behavioral limits that were broken by the children. In Chris's mind, he "just knew Mom would now need his help."

Guidelines for Caring Adults

Well-meaning adults sometimes encourage this forced sense of maturity on a bereaved child because they find it easier to respond to the child at this inappropriate level. In its extreme form, the surviving parent may even attempt (consciously or unconsciously) to have the child literally serve as a replacement for the dead spouse. When this situation occurs, the child's self-identity and self-esteem frequently are negatively influenced. Long-term depression often results.

◆ **Be aware of the potential negative impact that trite comments can have on a bereaved child.**
Caring adults can take a major step in preventing these potentially serious hyper-mature behaviors by not handing out trite, damaging advice like, "Now you have to be the man of the house." For adults, the goal should be to work with guided compassion to help bereaved children and their families experience as normal as possible matura-tional development patterns following the death of someone loved.

VI
Sarah Experiences Explosive Emotions

On occasion, Sarah would pause to reflect on those things that she missed the most since the death of her beloved father: "Not having my daddy to hug me and hold me . . . Not having our special Saturday time to be alone together

. . . Not hearing his voice anymore.''

Yes, Sarah missed her loving father, and, like most bereaved children, expressed her grief in a variety of ways. On one particular day, however, she suddenly experienced an outburst of explosive emotional behavior—a startling, yet normal, response to the death of her beloved father.

Even as she entered the classroom, Sarah knew it would be a difficult day. Five months had passed since the tragic car accident, and now spring was arriving. The grass was turning green, and the flowers were beginning to bloom.

During morning recess, Sarah turned to one of her best friends and said, "My daddy loved the springtime. We worked in the garden together, and he made me laugh." Fortunately, the teacher overheard Sarah and would remember these words later in the day.

After lunch, the teacher asked the class to open their spelling books. As her classmates opened their books, Sarah stared blankly out the window. She wasn't moving, she wasn't talking, she wasn't listening. Her third-grade teacher, Mrs. Miller, noticed Sarah seemed to be somewhere else. In a gentle tone, she called out to this eight-year-old child, "Sarah, can you get out your spelling book?"

That was all Sarah needed to hear. Without a moment's hesitation, she bolted from her chair and headed for the door. Again, her teacher spoke to her, "Sarah, can you talk to me?"

Once again, Sarah didn't say a word as she moved quickly toward an outdoor exit. In an effort to stop her, the teacher raised her tone of voice and said, "Stop, you can't go out there by yourself."

Sarah stopped in her tracks, turned to face her teacher and yelled in rage, "I hate you and I hate school. Just leave me alone."

Sarah was angry and she didn't care who knew it. Another third grade teacher had heard the commotion and entered the hallway. Mr. Williams was between Sarah and the outside exit.

Mrs. Miller asked her fellow teacher to keep Sarah from leaving the building. As he reached out to stop her, Sarah lashed out again, "Go away and leave me alone!" With one teacher standing in front of her, and one teacher behind her, Sarah not only felt alone and angry, she felt trapped.

Sarah sat down right in the middle of the hallway. Tightening her fists, she began to beat her hands on the floor's hard surface. Her anger soon turned to hurt as she began to sob tears that reflected her innermost feelings.

Sarah's compassionate teacher slowly moved toward her. Upon reaching this teary-eyed little girl, she knelt down, wrapped her in her arms, and gently embraced her. Five minutes passed without a word being spoken.

Slowly, and with some hesitation, Sarah peered into Mrs. Miller's eyes and spoke, "I miss my daddy so much. I'm sorry I'm so mad all the time. I just wish he could be here so we could have a garden this year...Mommy says we can still have a garden, but it won't be the same without my daddy."

Mrs. Miller leaned closer and softly said, "Sarah, you loved your daddy very much, and he loved you. You miss him and sometimes you get mad. That's all right. Let's just sit here together for awhile. Maybe you can tell me what you and your daddy used to plant in the garden."

A Counselor's Perspective. . .

Naturally, bereaved children experience a variety of thoughts and feelings as they participate in the "work of mourning." As caring adults, we should never prescribe what children's experiences will be, but instead allow them to "teach us" what their unique journeys into grief are like for them.

Sarah, like many other grieving children, outwardly expressed one part of her "grief work" with explosive emotions. In her situation, all it took was the onset of spring—a special time for Sarah and her daddy.

Explosive emotions can be upsetting and threatening to adults because they are often uncertain how to respond to the child's expression of these complex feelings. Sometimes adults oversimplify these emotions by talking only about anger. The bereaved child, however, may also experience feelings of hate, blame, terror, resentment, rage, and jealousy. While each of these emotions has distinctive features, enough similarities exist to warrant discussing them together.

Underneath her outward expression of

explosive emotions, Sarah was experiencing the more primary feelings of pain, helplessness, frustration, fear, and hurt. The primary responsibility for caring adults is to become aware of the significance of these underlying feelings behind the child's explosive emotional behavior.

Explosive emotions often express a child's desire to restore things to the way they were before the death. Even though the bereaved child is aware of the death, this behavior often expresses a desire to bring back the person who has died. Anger and other related emotions, however, are a grieving child's natural, intelligent response to the death of someone loved and an effort to restore a valued relationship that has been lost.

Explosive emotional behavior may also signal a bereaved child's anger at the person who died because, as the child views the situation, "If Daddy loved me enough, he wouldn't have died and left me." The child may then further reason, "If Dad doesn't love me, no one can love me. There must be something about me that makes me unlovable."

A bereaved child's anger and rage may be directed toward anyone available: surviving parent, teacher, playmates, God, or the world in general. As part of this behavior, some bereaved children may even be testing the idea if they should ever love again. The rationale — if they love anyone again, that person may die, too.

The fact that the dead person does not come back, despite the child's explosive emotions, is actually a part of the reality testing necessary for eventual healing to occur. With the gradual awareness that the person who died will not return, a child's need to express these explosive emotions will typically change.

As a counselor, my experiences with hundreds of bereaved children has also taught me an important lesson: there is a healthy survival value in being able to temporarily protest the painful reality of the loss. Having the capacity to express anger gives a child the courage to survive during a difficult time. Children who do not give themselves permission to protest, or do not receive permission from other people to do so, may slide into chronic depression. They are literally deprived of a means of psychological survival.

Adults who have difficulty allowing children to express their explosive emotions often operate on the following premise: "If the child is angry at me, something must be wrong with either him or me." As a result, these adults may do everything they can to keep the child from expressing anger.

After the death of someone loved, however, children are very perceptive. They often quickly notice adults' intolerance for the expression of anger. As a result, children may begin to feel guilty about their anger. Some bereaved children also are taught that to "be good" means never to express anger, regardless of the circumstances.

Unfortunately, these bereaved children who repress or deny their explosive feelings will turn their anger inward. The painful result is often low self-esteem, depression, chronic feelings of guilt, and physical complaints. When anger is directed inward, the bereaved child's experience with grief often becomes complicated and confusing.

Guidelines for Caring Adults

The major role of caring adults when a child

demonstrates explosive emotional behavior is to be a supportive stabilizer. Adults need to tolerate, encourage, and validate explosive emotions without judging, retaliating, or arguing.

While it is normal for an adult to experience an urge to "fight or flee" when anyone expresses anger, neither response is helpful to the bereaved child. The caring presence of a non-judgmental adult, however, is helpful and often allows the child to release his or her pent-up emotions. As a supportive stabilizer, an adult can validate these emotions and help the child explore them.

A word of caution: never attempt to prescribe what these emotions should be for a bereaved child. Simply be alert for them. Let the child "teach you" if explosive emotions are part of his or her grief experience. In some situations, such as when a death is anticipated, the demonstration of explosive emotions may be only mild or completely nonexistent.

♦ **Encourage the healthy expression of a child's explosive emotions so these feelings will be expressed, not repressed.**

Avoid inducing feelings of guilt in a child who expresses these complex emotions. Through permissive listening, the bereaved child will learn that these feelings are not judged by adults as being good or bad, right or wrong. The child learns that these feelings are just accepted.

◆ **Remember that explosive emotional behavior often signals the child's underlying feelings of pain, helplessness, frustration, fear, and hurt.**
During this difficult time, caring adults need to "be with" and support the grieving child as he or she does the painful work of mourning.

Mrs. Miller skillfully demonstrated to Sarah that anger and other explosive emotions, while often irrational, can be a normal and natural part of a child's grief experience. Adults who fail to realize this fact can leave a child feeling abandoned, guilty, and confused.

Caring adults recognize the need to provide the bereaved child with a safe place to be angry.

While doing the work of mourning, the child most benefits from stabilizing and sustaining relationships. Adults have the opportunity and privilege of creating such relationships.

VII
Sarah's
Acting-Out
Behavior

Sarah put her hand on the railing and slowly descended the stairs. But halfway down, something caught her attention. She felt a tightness in her throat. Sitting at the foot of the steps was her mother.

Mom was embracing a picture of Dad as she softly cried tears of sadness. Seeing Mommy cry naturally touched her own feelings of loss. Tears began to roll down Sarah's face as Mom looked up from the picture.

Heartbeats were measured in hours as their eyes made contact. Mrs. Johnson spoke first. "It's okay Sarah, I'm just missing your daddy. Do you want to sit with me?"

As Sarah snuggled up next to her mother, she responded in a faltering voice, "I miss Daddy so much. I just wish he could come home." Yes, this petite eight-year-old was in the midst of a very personal journey of grief.

It didn't seem possible that six months had passed since her daddy's tragic death in the car accident. After a brief pause Sarah continued, "Sometimes when I'm coming home from school, I think I'll find out Daddy has come back."

These honest hopes brought more tears for both mother and daughter. Mrs. Johnson swallowed hard before responding. "Yes, Sarah . . . I guess we sometimes wish we could just wake up and find out this was all a bad dream."

But this painful experience was not a dream; it was reality. The ebbs and flows of grief were an integral part of this family's daily life. The

Johnsons, however, had come to understand that shared grief results in movement toward healing.

They would ultimately come to know that grief does not "go away," but that as human beings they would learn to "live with" their grief. And while they were not yet far enough into their journey to realize it, days of hope for purpose and value in living would eventually return. Right now, daily survival was the task at hand.

Just the day before, for example, two of Sarah's favorite cousins had come over for an afternoon of fun and play. Nine-year-old Phil and seven-year-old Anne were talking on Sarah's toy telephones.

At first, Sarah thought her cousins' phone play was just fine. The only problem was that they were having such a great time that they decided not to let Sarah play with them.

With little need for provocation, Sarah suddenly grabbed one of the phones from Anne as she knocked her cousin to the ground. Without hesitation, Sarah jumped on top of Anne and began to hit her on the arms and *chest. Anne began to cry and scream.*

Mrs. Johnson heard the cries from the kitchen. As she peered out the bay window, she could see Sarah hitting Anne. Quickly, she moved toward the backyard.

When she reached Sarah, she gently pulled her off her cousin. Sarah was still raging and throwing her arms about. Mrs. Johnson took three steps backward as she began to speak, "Sarah, you can be angry at Anne, but there will be no hurting. People are not for hurting."

A Counselor's Perspective. . .

Many bereaved children express the pain of grief through "acting-out behaviors." The specific acting-out behavior usually varies depending on the child's age and developmental level. Fighting with her cousin was just one example of how Sarah acted out her grief.

A bereaved child may have temper outbursts, become unusually loud and noisy, initiate fights with other children or adults, defy authority, or simply rebel against everything and everybody. Other examples of acting-out behavior include getting poor grades in school, or assuming a general attitude of "I don't care about anything." Older children may even run away from home.

Understanding and appropriately responding to the bereaved child's acting out may seem like an ominous task. Broken down into component parts, however, it is not so overwhelming. To begin with, it is important to understand why bereaved children act out in the first place. A number of factors influence this behavior.

Feelings of Insecurity

Bereaved children naturally experience a sense of insecurity following the death of someone loved. After all, the family — often the most stabilizing influence in their lives — has experienced the loss of one of its members. Acted-out feelings unconsciously provide the child with a sense of control and power.

While Sarah's fighting with her cousin doesn't achieve a solution to her daddy's death, it does provide her with a temporary sense of strength. While outside observers might judge that she is "out of control," Sarah is actually trying to "gain some control."

Temper outbursts or fighting are also

frightening to the other person involved in the conflict. This fear response often contributes to the bereaved child's experience of a temporary sense of power or control. Obviously, however, being aware of this phenomenon does not mean adults should ignore the consequences of this behavior. Adults must set appropriate limits while at the same time recognizing the possible reasons for the child's actions.

Feelings of Abandonment

Bereaved children may feel as if their dead parent has abandoned or "died on them." Consequently, they sometimes feel unloved; their self-esteem is affected. As a result, some bereaved children will act out because they feel unloved. The acting-out behaviors create a self-fulfilling prophecy, such as, "See, nobody loves me."

A Desire to Provoke Punishment

Even though it is not rational to adults, some bereaved children reason that "If I'm so bad that somebody I loved died, then I deserve to be punished." Again, this reasoning is usually an unconscious process of which the child is unaware.

The parent who died may also have been the primary disciplinarian within the family. Consequently, this acting-out behavior may be an attempt to retrieve or get the parent to "come back." The rationale often goes as follows: "If I'm bad, Dad will have to come back and make me behave."

Protection From Future Losses

Bereaved children sometimes become the initiators of rejection in an effort to prevent feelings of "abandonment" in the future. Their acting-out behaviors serve to keep people at a distance. The result—they become the ones who control the situation where loss is experienced rather than passively suffer the possibility of being left again.

Essentially, the bereaved child unconsciously reasons that it is better to be the abandoner than the abandoned. Acting-out behavior protects the child from intimate relationships and protects them from the additional hurt and pain encountered when another loss occurs.

Demonstration of Internal Feelings of Grief

Unfortunately, many bereaved children grieve but do not mourn. As clinically defined, grief is the collective thoughts and feelings about a loss that are within oneself; mourning is the sharing of these thoughts and feelings outside of oneself. In other words, mourning is "grief gone public."

Bereaved children are often referred to as the "forgotten mourners." Some people assume children are too young to need to talk out their thoughts and feelings of grief. The result—many children grieve, but do not mourn. Feelings build up inside a child with no way to be expressed outwardly.

As these thoughts and feelings go unexpressed, they continue to fester within. A bereaved child's internal agitation builds. Ultimately, however, the stress erupts—one way or another. Acting-out behaviors are often seen in children who have been grieving, but not mourning outside of themselves. Bereaved children experience many thoughts, feelings, and behaviors while doing the work of mourning. If acting-out behavior is a part of a child's grief experience, caring adults need to be prepared to respond in healthy, life-enhancing ways.

Adult Response to Acting-out Behaviors

Acting-out behavior in bereaved children is often an indirect, unconscious cry for help. Perhaps no area of bereavement care is more sophisticated and complex than appropriately understanding and responding to acting-out behaviors.

Much debate exists about how an adult should best respond to a child who acts out. When the child is bereaved, this debate becomes even more complex. Some people tend to over-discipline; others become permissive to the degree that the child "takes over."

Healthy limit-setting by caring adults helps a bereaved child grow. In other words, adults must work to understand what function the acting-out behavior serves in the child. This basic recognition is the essence of artfully helping during this difficult time.

Adults should first ask, "What are the genuine needs of a bereaved child who acts out?" My experience as a grief counselor has shown that probably the two greatest needs of a bereaved child are for affection and a sense of security. Appropriate discipline should then attempt to meet these essential needs related to love and care. In doing so, adults should help the bereaved child know in his or her head and heart that "I am lovable in spite of my present behavior."

Too many times, bereaved children are punished in ways that are counterproductive. Adult disciplinary responses must respect the unique personality of each child. Discipline and limit-setting must communicate to the child that adults recognize and accept these individual qualities and love the child despite the misbehavior.

Unfortunately, some adults attempt to set limits on acting-out behavior while communicating to the child that he or she is a "bad boy" or "bad girl." The message is often, "You are being punished because you are bad." In this example, no distinction is made between inappropriate behavior and being a bad person.

Bereaved children should never be made to feel they are bad. Using "goodness" and "badness" as distinct alternatives is inappropriate and usually results in long-term, negative consequences for the child.

When Sarah hit her cousin in order to retrieve a play telephone, obviously she needed to be stopped. Beyond that, however, she needed to be reassured that what she did was human and not a final judgment of her character. Sarah needed to feel that she was still lovable, despite her actions. Like Sarah, many bereaved children are being most unlovable when, in fact, they are seeking love and attention.

In an earlier situation, Sarah told her teacher, "I hate you, and I hate school. Just leave me alone." Though the teacher might have informed Sarah that she was a "bad girl" and sent her to the principal's office, instead she knelt down, wrapped Sarah in her arms and gently embraced her. What Sarah needed most of all while she was acting "unlovable" was understanding and nonjudgment.

Adult modeling and setting reasonable boundaries help bereaved children like Sarah develop their internal controls while at the same time still providing children the opportunity to make some painful mistakes. Discovering that we make mistakes as we grow up is an important ingredient of discipline. Mistakes are often one of the best sources of learning.

Special circumstances, like a death in the family, call for additional leeway with mistake-making behavior. These behavioral mistakes may include hitting a cousin, yelling at a teacher, or simply rebelling against everything and everybody. Caring adults do not have to like this behavior but tolerate it knowing the behavior reflects a child's hard times and new adjustments. Bereaved children need to be allowed to make mistakes while still maintaining the support, love, and understanding of adults.

When Sarah could not control the impulse to hit her cousin, she needed to know that someone older and wiser would intervene. To allow her to continue to hit her cousin would have only served to perpetuate the acting out. In addition, Sarah would not have learned the important distinction between understanding a feeling and taking an overt action.

Guidelines for Caring Adults

- **Set reasonable guidelines for bereaved children based on the type of acting-out**

behavior.

Setting limits on bereaved children who act out usually involves two behavioral issues: explosive feelings and explosive actions. Each part has to be responded to differently. Feelings have to be identified and expressed; actions may have to be limited and re-directed.

When Sarah's mother had to pull her daughter off cousin Anne, she said, "Sarah, you can be angry at Anne, but there will be no hurting. People are not for hurting!" The angry feeling was identified, but the act was limited. The limits were also set in a manner that preserved self-respect for Sarah.

♦ **Set limits without demonstrating anger or using violence.**

The limits described in the above paragraph were set without extreme anger or use of violence. And while Sarah's resentment of the limits might have been anticipated and understood, Mrs. Johnson did not punish Sarah additionally for not liking the limits.

♦ **Recognize that adult discipline will eventually lead to self-discipline.**

When handled appropriately, adult assistance with establishing external controls often leads the bereaved child to voluntary self-control and to changing certain behaviors. By identifying with respected adults and the values they teach, the bereaved child often develops inner standards for self-regulation of acting-out behavior.

As mentioned previously, how to respond to a bereaved child's acting-out behavior is probably one of the most difficult things for caring adults to understand. During the past few years, I have collected questions that workshop participants have asked regarding this issue. These questions and answers are included in the Appendix section of this book. Please keep in mind that my responses to the questions are designed to be suggestions, not instructions.

VIII
Sarah
Feels Guilty
About Her
Father's
Death

To Sarah, the first eight months of her bereavement sometimes seemed like three years. At other times, it seemed like the death of her father happened only yesterday. Time passed differently now that her daddy wasn't around to take her places and play with her.

Just this last week, Sarah's Grandpa had taken her out for dinner. Grandpa was a good listener, and he let Sarah talk about whatever was on her mind. Actually, she discovered that Grandpa was one of the few people she liked to talk with about her daddy.

They had been eating and visiting for a while when all of a sudden Sarah said, "Grandpa, why didn't I make my dad stay at home that day?" Sarah's question had been inside her head for a long time. Only now, in the security of being with her favorite grandpa, could she talk about what was bothering her.

Grandpa was a wise man. He realized that Sarah needed to "talk out" her feelings about her father's death. Instead of rushing in with a quick answer, he let Sarah talk about how she wished she could have prevented her dad's death in the auto accident.

While continuing to encourage Sarah to talk, he slowly shared the following comment, "Yes, Sarah, I know that if there were anything you or I could have done, we would have done it. Sometimes things happen that we can't always control."

Grandpa was only beginning to help Sarah come to understand that there are certain things in life that cannot be controlled. He knew that to simply reassure Sarah and not let her talk about her thoughts and feelings would ultimately make her feel powerless.

A Counselor's Perspective. . .

At some point, most children have wished their parents would go away and leave them alone. So when a parent dies, the child may well assume blame for thinking these thoughts and, as a consequence, feel guilty.

Bereaved children may blame themselves for any number of things from being bad to having been angry with the person who died. As a result, some children feel total responsibility for the death, yet say nothing to anyone about this feeling. Instead, they may become chronically depressed or have multiple physical complaints.

Attempting to Control the Uncontrollable

By asking Grandpa, "Why didn't I make my daddy stay home that day?" Sarah was attempting to control the uncontrollable. Asking this question reflects Sarah's feelings of guilt and self-blame related to the death of her father.

Children naturally feel helpless when someone they love has died. Regardless of how irrational these feelings may seem to outside observers, if a child believes he or she was the cause—that something he or she did or didn't do made the death occur—it naturally follows that if the child had done something different, the person would still be alive.

The bereaved child may think or say: "I'm a bad person for what I have (or have not) done." As a result, the child sometimes feels the need to be punished, or actually seek out forms of self-punishment. Acting-out behavior is often influenced by the child's belief that he or she caused the death to occur and should be punished.

When children feel helpless, they may attempt to gain some sense of control by thinking that if they had done something differently, the person would not have died. In other words, if children see themselves as being the cause, they think there well may be something they could do to bring the person back to life.

Attempting to control the uncontrollable often also reflects a child's experience of explosive emotions about the death. When anger is directed at the person who has died, a bereaved child may become confused and internalize unspoken thoughts such as, "How can I be mad at somebody I love? There must be something wrong with me."

Communicating to bereaved children that explosive emotions are inappropriate can occur directly or indirectly. Some adults may specifically tell a child that he or she should never be angry. This is particularly true if the adult is threatened by his or her own anger. When adults never express their own explosive emotions, they become models for children not to express their angry feelings either.

Survival Guilt and Relief

Surviving a person who has died, particularly a parent, brother or sister, sometimes generates feelings of guilt in bereaved children. The child observes, for example, the other parent's pain and reasons, "Maybe it should have been me instead of my father." What the child may not realize is that if he or she had died, the parent would be experiencing the same pain of grief. Caring adults must stay alert to the need to explore this phenomenon with bereaved children.

Relief-Guilt Syndrome

Another type of guilt may evolve when a person's death brings a child some sense of relief or release. This situation often occurs when the person who died had been ill for a long period of time or the child's relationship with the person who died was in conflict.

After a long illness, a child may not miss the frequent trips to the hospital or how the family always focused on the dying person. If the bereaved child is not able to acknowledge this sense of relief as natural and not equal to a lack of love, he or she may feel guilty for feeling relieved.

Personality Factors and Guilt

Another form of guilt evolves from long-standing personality factors within the bereaved child. Some children are taught early in life that when anything bad or unfortunate occurs, it is their fault. Consequently, when a death occurs, they look first within themselves to find blame. This kind of guilt becomes an ingrained part of their character development.

These children definitely need the context of a professional counseling relationship to make constructive changes. Unfortunately, these children often live in families where outside help is not made available.

Guilt and Punishment

Some bereaved children anticipate that punishment (from outside or inside) should result from experiencing feelings of guilt. As a consequence, adults might witness children who attempt to lessen their guilt with punishment. They may directly or indirectly ask to be punished.

Obviously, seeking out punishment is self-destructive and only makes the child's situation worse. For caring adults, the task is to help the bereaved child feel less guilty and thus reduce his or her need to demonstrate self-destructive behaviors. These children often are also accident-prone and exhibit a high level of risk-taking behavior. Seeking professional help is valuable when a child is consumed by guilt and endangers his or her personal safety.

Joy-Guilt Syndrome

A bereaved child can also experience feelings of guilt when he or she begins to re-experience any kind of joy or happiness in life. These feelings often relate to a sense of loyalty to the person who died and a fear that being happy in some way betrays that relationship. Opportunities to explore these feelings are necessary as the child moves forward in his or her grief experience.

Final Thoughts About A Child's Feelings of Guilt

Because guilt often provides a bereaved child with the feeling of being able to control or sometimes even reverse the death, he or she does not just let go of these thoughts. To give up the regret or guilt would be to acknowledge deep feelings of helplessness. The child simply may not want to do that yet. Only in the security of nonjudgmental, compassionate adults will some bereaved children fully acknowledge the depth of their hurt and pain.

Sarah has come to realize that she could talk about anything with her grandpa. As time passed, he would continue to listen and learn about her needs. He would also help her realize that there are certain things in life that cannot be controlled. For example, Sarah would come to realize she could control things like what she ate, when she went to bed, or what she wore to school.

Sarah would also learn to understand that she could not control the rain, wind, lightning, or the sunrise. Also, Sarah could not control the death of her beloved father. Children must be helped to understand this sad, but true, reality. Caring adults, like Grandpa, can help children actively do the "work of mourning" and at the same time rediscover the joy of continued living and loving. With Grandpa's support, eventually Sarah will understand it was not her fault that her daddy died.

IX
Sarah
Experiences
"Grief Attacks"

It had been sixteen months since Sarah's daddy died in the auto accident that forever changed the course of this little girl's life.

Some adults around Sarah mistakenly assumed that she should "be over" her grief by now. Recently, a well-intentioned, but misinformed, adult had said to Sarah, "Well, now you need to get on with your life."

Sarah was beginning to understand that grief was like waves coming in off the ocean. Sometimes the waves were small, while at other times, they came crashing in and pulled her feet right out from under her.

A huge wave had hit Sarah one week. She was in her bedroom cleaning out the bottom of her closet. Mom had asked all of the children to help with a major cleanup of each of their bedrooms. This was a task that Sarah didn't want to do in the first place; but, following Mom's request, she slowly cleaned through the mess at the bottom of her closet.

She was almost finished when all of a sudden she picked up a little airplane. This model airplane had special meaning to Sarah. Dad and she had shared a special secret: someday they would take flying lessons together.

As tears filled her eyes, she remembered a special day only a few weeks before her dad's death. He had picked her up after school on a sunny afternoon, and they had gone out to the local airport to watch the planes take off and land.

She remembered how they talked of learning to fly together and how much fun that would be. They smiled at each other as the planes came and went. Now, as Sarah sat quietly on the floor of her closet, she began to cry out in pain. This little girl missed her daddy so much.

As she cried, she recalled how on the way home that sunny afternoon, Dad and she had stopped at a hobby shop. Together, they picked out a model airplane. It had seats for just two people. They went right home and put the airplane together on the kitchen table. She had felt so very close to her father that day.

As Sarah held the airplane with both hands, she sobbed uncontrollably. Between the tears, she cried out, "I miss my daddy." Alone in her closet, Sarah embraced a sense of loss and loneliness that she had never experienced before.

Sarah's mom was not in the house to hear Sarah's tears of sadness. Sarah cried non-stop for twenty minutes as she sat motionless in the closet. Slowly, this new wave of grief began to lessen and she looked forward to telling her mom about what happened. She knew that Mom would try as best she could to help her with her airplane memories.

A Counselor's Perspective. . .

Yes, sometimes all it takes is a small airplane to trigger a child's grief. And these "grief attacks" come when least expected. At other times, bereaved children feel the waves of grief are flowing toward them. In either case, the full sense of loss never occurs all at once. Months, sometimes years, may pass before a child is confronted by how much his or her life has been changed by the death.

Grief attacks, or times of intense feelings of loss, emptiness, and sadness, are naturally difficult times for bereaved children.

When these intense feelings occur, children are often very frightened. Thinking and hoping that the most devastating of emotions have already occurred, they are usually unprepared for the depth of the experience.

If given the opportunity, bereaved children can teach adults about grief attacks. During my years of experience as a counselor, children have taught me that the following times can often trigger "grief attacks": birthdays (their own or the person's who died); starting or getting out of school for the year; receiving a report card; holidays; vacations; weekends; returning home to an empty house; their first date; graduating from school; getting married; any kind of anniversary.

The unexpected waves usually come out of nowhere and are stimulated by a sight, a sound or a smell. These senses trigger intense feelings of loss and sadness. Unless children share these experiences with someone, they can and often do suffer in silence. Keep in mind — children have the right to experience these intense feelings of loss, emptiness and sadness. Unfortunately, many well-meaning adults try to take these feelings away. Friends, family, and even some professional caregivers often believe their jobs are to distract children rather than help them embrace these feelings.

Adult caregivers often worry about depression in the bereaved child. Naturally, as children struggle with this heightened sense of loss, they become depressed. And rightfully so! The death of someone loved is something about which to be depressed. The key, however, is that the intensity and duration of the depression should lessen over time as the child is allowed to do the "work of mourning."

Clinical Depression vs. Normal Grief Attacks

Perhaps it would be helpful to note some differences between clinical depression and the normal depressive experience of grief. Realizing that caregivers may use differing criteria, the following are some of the distinctions I find helpful to distinguish between depressive grief in children and other forms of depression.

- In normal grief, children respond to comfort and support; clinically depressed children often reject support.

- The bereaved child is often able to use play to work out feelings of grief; the depressed child is more often resistant to the use of play.

- The bereaved child is often openly angry; the depressed child may complain and be irritable, but may not directly express anger.

- Bereaved children will usually connect depressed feelings to the loss they have experienced; depressed children often do not relate their experiences to any life event.

- In normal grief, bereaved children can still experience moments of enjoyment in life; depressed children often project a pervasive sense of doom.

- Caring adults around the bereaved child can sense feelings of sadness and emptiness; the depressed child often projects a sense of hopelessness and chronic emptiness.

- While the bereaved child is more likely to have transient physical complaints, the depressed child may have chronic physical complaints.

◆ Bereaved children may express guilt over some specific aspect of the loss; depressed children often have generalized feelings of guilt.

◆ While the self-esteem of bereaved children is temporarily impacted, it is usually not the depth of loss of esteem typically seen in clinically depressed children.

Obviously, it is not always easy to distinguish between the depression of grief and chronic forms of depression in children. If caring adults have doubts or concerns about this difference, they would probably be well-served to seek help from someone who specializes in this area of care.

Guidelines for Caring Adults

When children like Sarah experience intense feelings of loss and sadness, they need the frequent and regular presence of a supportive and stabilizing adult. Grief attacks can be extremely frightening to children. For adult caregivers, helping means not allowing children to feel alone as they struggle with these feelings.

Many children will not initiate talking about their grief attacks. They often, however, give indirect cues. When these urgent cues are not heard or are misunderstood, the result is often another experience of loss for the bereaved child.

- **Encourage the child to talk about his or her intense feelings.**

  When ready, the child should be encouraged to share these intense feelings. An important person in the child's life has died, and a precious memory still exists in the child's mind.

  At times, children find it easier to express such intense feelings through play, art forms, or writing. During these times, the child may review events both before and after the death. And each time the child talks about the death, it becomes a little more bearable.

- **Do not shut off the child's grief in an effort to protect your own emotions.**

  Perhaps the biggest key for adults is to "be

with" children during this painful time rather than trying to minimize the experience to protect themselves. Adults should also avoid trying to "do something" for a child during a grief attack. Caring adults can model the expression of their own grief attacks as a way of normalizing the child's experience.

No, children don't always have a supportive adult available when they have a grief attack. If they know of loving and gentle support, however, they will often be able to later share these lonely experiences.

X
Sarah
And
Reconciliation

Sarah came up the stairs in the Center for Loss and Life Transition and entered my office. I was so happy to see her. It had been about three months since Sarah and I had last visited.

The time had come for Sarah's "check-up." Almost three-and-a-half years had passed since Sarah's father died in an automobile accident. Without saying any words, we gave each other a hug, and our eyes exchanged a special look. She knew I wanted to listen and learn from her — and she had been such a great teacher!

As I realized our work together was coming to an end, I felt sad. But graduation from a counseling relationship is a necessary part of healing. I knew I would need to talk to a colleague about my own feelings of loss and sadness.

Now I was ready to continue learning as

Sarah shared her ongoing journey with me. She was enthusiastic as she told me about her swimming lessons. I had to laugh as she informed me that she could probably out-race me. This was kind of an inside joke, because whenever we played games, she invariably won!

She quickly turned toward the play area that takes up a portion of my office. As she grabbed the walkie-talkies, I knew we were going to play our memory game.

Early in our counseling, Sarah and I discovered we worked well when we visited this way. We called it our game of "Memory Embrace." It was not only fun, it seemed to help her enable me to understand her experience.

As Sarah and I went down two flights of stairs and out into the Colorado sunshine, my two Siberian Huskies, Tasha and Kisha, greeted us with wagging tails. Sarah immediately hiked off into the trees on the south side of the building, while I moved off to the north side.

I had just found a log to sit on when Sarah's clear voice came booming over the walkie-talkie, "Are you ready to talk about memories?" She was getting right to work, so I tried to tune in *as best I could.*

"Yes, Sarah, I'm ready." She loved to talk about her father.

"I want to remember my mountain hikes with Daddy," Sarah explained with excitement.

"Okay, I'll listen and you talk." Without hesitation she began to relate one of her favorite memories. She called it her "Lake Agnes" story. The title came from their hike destination just the spring before her dad died. As they climbed the mountain to get to the lake, they had a discussion about "Why do people climb mountains?"

She recalled the hike as if it were yesterday. I still marvel at her attention to detail. Her favorite part of the story came right after she and her daddy had finished a long discussion. Suddenly, he had looked her right in the eye and said, "Sarah, I'd sure like to know why you think people climb mountains?"

Without hesitation she replied, "So they can be with their daddies!"

Yes, though Sarah continues to miss her daddy with all her heart, she was able to go on to teach me that in many ways her life was once again full of joy and excitement. Some people might think she was "over" her grief, but she wasn't. Children and adults alike don't "get over" grief, they live with it.

A Counselor's Perspective. . .

The final dimension of grief is often referred to as resolution, recovery, re-establishment, or reorganization. This dimension often suggests a total return to normalcy. Yet in my personal and professional experiences, everyone (whether adult or child) is changed by the experience of grief. To assume that life will be exactly as it was prior to the death is unrealistic and potentially damaging. Recovery too often is seen erroneously as an absolute, a perfect state of re-establishment.

"Reconciliation" is a term I believe better expresses what occurs as a bereaved child works to integrate the new reality of moving forward in life without the physical presence of the person who died. The child experiences a renewed sense of energy and confidence, an ability to fully acknowledge the reality of the death, and the capacity to become re-involved with the activities of living. He or she also acknowledges that pain and grief are difficult, yet necessary, parts of life and living.

As the experience of reconciliation unfolds, a child recognizes that life will be different without the person who has died. There is also an awareness that reconciliation is a process, not an event. Completing the emotional relationship with the person who has died and redirecting energy and initiative toward the future takes longer and involves more labor than most people realize.

A bereaved child's specific course of mourning cannot be prescribed. It depends on many factors, including the nature of the relationship with the person who died, the availability and helpfulness of a support system, the nature of the death, and the ritual of the funeral experience. Despite all that we have learned about childhood dimensions of grief, these dimensions will take different forms with different children.

In reconciliation, the full reality of the death becomes a part of the child. Beyond an intellectual working through grows an emotional working through. What has been understood at the "head" level is now understood at the "heart" level—the person who was loved is dead. When reminders such as holidays, anniversaries or other special memories are triggered, the child may experience the same pain inherent in grief, yet the duration and intensity of the pain are typically less severe as reconciliation occurs.

The pain changes from being ever-present, sharp, and stinging to a feeling of loss that has renewed meaning and purpose. The sense of loss does not completely disappear, but softens; the intense pangs of grief become less frequent. Hope for a continued life emerges as the child is able to make commitments to the future. There is a realization that the dead person will never be forgotten, along with the assurance that the child's own life can and will move forward.

The following information is a summary of the reconciliation criteria that will indicate to caring adults that a bereaved child has participated in the work of mourning and is emerging as a whole and healthy individual.

Those children who have approached the dimension of reconciliation should usually demonstrate the ability to accomplish the following:

— Recognize the reality and finality of the death of the person who has died.

— Return to stable eating and sleeping patterns that were present prior to the death.

— Experience a renewed sense of energy and personal well-being.

— Feel a sense of release or relief from the person who died (the child will continue to think about the person who died but not be preoccupied with these thoughts).

— Develop the capacity to enjoy experiences in life that are normally enjoyable.

— Establish new and healthy relationships.

— Live a full life without experiencing feelings of guilt or lack of self-respect.

— Adjust to the new role changes that have resulted from the loss of the relationship.

— Develop the capacity to be compassionate with oneself when normal grief attacks occur, such as on holidays, anniversaries, or special occasions.

— Develop the capacity to acknowledge that the pain of loss is an inherent part of life that results from the ability to give and receive love.

These criteria are intended to help caring adults assess a bereaved child's movement toward reconciliation. Not every child will illustrate each of these criteria. The majority of them, however, should be present to consider that the child is reconciling his or her loss.

Guidelines for Caring Adults

Movement toward reconciliation is draining and exhausting, not only for children but also for caregivers who accompany them on the journey. In a general sense, the major helping task of the adult caregiver is to be supportively present and assist the child to "stay on track."

Establishing the hope of reconciliation is central to the ultimate achievement of reconciliation. Many children experience a loss of confidence and self-esteem that leaves them questioning their capacity to heal. Those adult helpers who are able to embrace a willingness to hope and expect reconciliation empower the child to move toward their grief instead of away from it. This concept does not mean denying pain, but desiring to "be with" the child in his or her pain and helplessness—all the while knowing that wounds get worse before they get better.

Caring adults who expect reconciliation help a child to see it as a goal to work toward. Children need support, guidance, patience, perseverance, determination and perhaps most of all, hope and the belief in their capacity to heal. Part of the helping role is to serve as a catalyst that creates conditions outside the child and qualities within the child that make healing possible.

◆ **Embrace your own grief experiences while focusing on the child you are trying to help.**
Helping children move toward reconciliation means adults should be open to personal grief experiences, while keeping the focus on those they are attempting to help. Obviously, if the adult's grief becomes more important than working on that of the child, they render themselves impotent as helpers.

◆ **Do not impose your own direction on the content of what is explored as the child moves toward reconciliation.**

Adults should allow the direction of the child's growth to guide them as they respond in supportive, life-enhancing ways. Appreciate the child's independence and respect the right to determine the direction of his or her growth. From a therapeutic stance, caring adults should "follow the lead that is provided them."

The process of helping children restore and renew themselves calls upon all of the personal strengths of the adult helper. While working with children involved in the pain of grief is often difficult, slow and wearing, the work also can be enriching and fulfilling.

I believe it is a true honor to help children like Sarah find meaning in life following loss and transition. Reconciliation is essential if a child is to once again live a satisfying, enriched life. Only through the renewal of purpose and meaning can grief become an influence for growth in the life of the child.

XI
Saying
Good-Bye
To Sarah

Sarah's mom waited patiently in the library as Sarah continued to teach me. Before long, it was time to say goodbye. We decided to sit down with her mother and talk about if and when she would come to visit with me again.

After some important discussion, we decided she would come again in six months. Little by little, Sarah and I knew we were saying good-bye. Yet in my heart I know our mutual loss is a reflection of her healing and growth. I felt so honored to be a part of her journey.

APPENDIX
Adult Responses To Acting-Out Behavior

Question:

My husband died this past year. Does what I do with my "grief work" possibly influence acting-out behaviors in my children?

Response:

Absolutely! One of the most important influences on a child's capacity to mourn is what adults around them do with their own grief. For example, many bereaved children will unconsciously attempt to "act out" the thoughts and feelings of adults in their environment.

If your explosive emotions, for example, are repressed or denied, you may discover that your children will try to do your mourning for you. This behavior supports the premise that some bereaved children will even feel responsible for the reconciliation of their parent's grief.

Acting-out behaviors can also be used to

attempt to force re-engagement of an emotionally distant adult. If your child is worried about you, he or she may use acting-out behaviors as a way to distract and re-engage you.

As you do your "work of mourning," you will eventually become more emotionally available to your child. Give yourself permission to work on your own healing, and your child will feel more secure. As a result, he or she will have less of a need to use acting out as a way of gaining strength.

While you balance allowing yourself to mourn with staying emotionally connected to your child, realize another benefit. Your child will be less likely to fear closeness and push people away through acting-out behavior. As you and your child experience mutual love, he or she will be less in need of testing through acting-out behavior the fear that you, too, might die.

Question:

Does allowing myself to mourn actually help my child feel less of a need to act out grief?

Response:

Yes. As you do your work of mourning, you ultimately become more available to help your child heal in his or her grief. It is important never to conceal personal mourning from your child. Adults seem to instinctively want to protect children from pain. Understand, however, that perhaps no one is more perceptive to emotional climates than a bereaved child.

The key is helping children understand that they are not the cause of your grief. While you might be sad, the child needs to know this is not rejection. The result—the child will learn to talk about some of his or her frightening feelings without acting out in destructive ways.

Question:

Some well-meaning friends tell me I should "punish" my bereaved child's acting-out behaviors. Is disciplining or setting limits the same as punishment?

Response:

There is a distinction between discipline and punishment. Should you ever hear someone say,

"That child needs to be punished," the person probably does not understand the difference.

To discipline does not mean to punish, hurt, threaten or discourage. Actually, discipline means "to teach." Disciplining a child is hopefully a time of teaching, encouraging, and motivating the child to behave responsibly.

Bereaved children who act out are children who are discouraged. Obviously, a helpful approach to discouragement is encouragement. Discipline with encouragement means that you believe in the child's capacity to behave in positive ways. While the child may need your adult help in setting limits, your goal should never be seen as "punishing the child into submission."

Over the long term, the goal of disciplining a bereaved child is to ultimately enable the child to one day assume responsibility for his or her own self-discipline. If you succeed, be proud of yourself.

Question:

My wife died of cancer this past year. I sometimes get so frustrated at my nine-year-old son's behavior that I feel like spanking him. What are your thoughts about spanking?

Response:

The dreaded question: "To spank or not to spank?" The saying is that people do not believe in spanking until they have children of their own. Well, I have worked with hundreds of children in counseling, and I have children of my own, but I still don't believe that spanking is an effective or appropriate means of discipline.

Feeling a desire to spank and spanking, however, are two very different issues. When you are mourning, you may discover yourself wanting to get the discipline over quickly and efficiently. Yet social-learning theory teaches us that children look to adults as models for appropriate behavior. To model spanking only teaches children that physical force is an appropriate behavior. Furthermore, spanking establishes an emotional environment of associating love with violence. The child learns that it is acceptable for people who love each other to hit each other.

Spanking is not an encouraging method of

discipline. Instead, spanking tells the bereaved child that you don't like his or her present behavior, but it doesn't motivate responsible behavior. It also implies to the child that if you do not like someone's behavior, physical force is justifiable.

Spanking a child may stop a behavior, but what does it teach him or her about self-discipline? It simply teaches that if you are big, you can hit. Child-care specialist Dr. Arnold Gesell once suggested that if you plan to NEVER spank your child, you'll probably end up spanking about the right amount. I agree.

Question:

Does withholding information about the nature of the death potentially contribute to acting-out in bereaved children?

Response:

Yes. As a matter of fact, it is a much more common contributor to acting-out behaviors than most people realize. Adults who withhold important information about the nature of the death prevent children from moving toward reconciliation to the loss. Adults, however, should always provide information at children's level of comprehension.

Sharing relevant information about the death relates to the principle that "children can attempt to cope with what they know but often cannot cope with what they do not know." Acting-out behavior is sometimes an unconscious "searching" for the truth. Although children may be unable to completely understand the nature of the death, open and honest communication establishes a trusting relationship and helps prevent problems that can result when information is kept secret.

Question:

I sometimes get drawn into a need to lecture my child when he acts out. Is lecturing an appropriate means of preventing acting-out behavior?

Response:

The tendency to lecture your child just demonstrates that you are human. But, the answer to your question is "no." Lecturing rarely helps children reduce their acting-out behaviors. Usually, the bereaved child gets bored by any kind of lecturing and quickly tunes out the well-meaning adult.

Sometimes, children even appear to be listening, but they are actually in another world. And pleading or talking "at" them instead of "with" them creates more harm than good. In reality, lecturing may increase the child's acting-out because it proves the behavior is getting the adult's attention.

Question:

Do children realize they are hurting themselves when they act out behaviorally?

Response:

No, usually they don't. Their need to act out is so great that they blind themselves to any self-destructive results of this behavior. When the need to act out is so great, children have little capacity to perceive the self-destructive consequences. As caring adults, the task is to understand the need for the behavior, while at the same time setting appropriate limits.

Question:

Is it helpful to try to get children to "talk-out" what they feel?

Response:

Yes. Always keep in mind, however, that some children talk about their feelings more easily than others. If we remember that "discipline" means "to teach," we can help children learn to express whatever they might be feeling.

Children also sense that the adult who encourages the expression of feelings demonstrates some of the following qualities: a desire to understand; warmth and caring; acceptance; and trust. If these qualities are present, the bereaved child will often "teach you" what he or she is feeling inside. And once you understand the function the acting-out behavior serves, you can help the child heal.

Keep in mind — feelings of explosive emotions and underlying helplessness are often at the root of acting-out behavior. Regardless of the feelings, such as love, anger, sadness, or guilt, talking out and playing out these feelings seem to be critical ingredients to healing. If children are not allowed to express their feelings, the emotions do not simply go away. Bereaved children who are taught to repress feelings typically experience secondary symptoms of headaches, stomach pains, nervous tics, or other signs of internal stress.

Question:

Are there constructive ways to allow bereaved children to act out their feelings?

Response:

Absolutely! Physical activities such as sports are a common and socially acceptable way for children to express their feelings. Many bereaved children I have counseled became very involved in sports.

There are also a variety of other appropriate outlets for feelings, such as hitting a punching bag, painting pictures, dancing, or using puppets. Through these physical activities, children can understand and accept whatever feelings they are experiencing.

A Final Note:

These questions and responses are not intended to be all-inclusive. I have included them in this book to provide some helpful information for caring adults. Most importantly, I want to emphasize that adults must carefully observe and listen to acting-out behavior in bereaved children. By doing so, children will "teach us" what their needs are. Our task becomes one of hearing their cries for help and responding with both our heads and our hearts.